God's Plan for the Local Church

GOD'S PLAN FOR THE
LOCAL CHURCH

Nigel Lacey

Grace Publications

GRACE PUBLICATIONS TRUST
139 Grosvenor Avenue, London, N5 2NH, England.

© Nigel Lacey

First published 1985

ISBN 0 946462 07 0

Distributed by:
EVANGELICAL PRESS
16/18 High Street, Welwyn, Hertfordshire, AL6 9EQ, England

Cover and illustrations by Sandra Littleton Evans

Typeset by Berea Press, Glasgow, Scotland.
Printed by Ancor Brendon, Colchester, England.

Contents

Preface

During 1983, local church life and practice was the subject of the midweek Bible ministry at Bethesda, Stowmarket. The notes that accompanied the ministry were widely read and discussed and it was decided to incorporate them into a small book that might, in the goodness of God, be helpful to a wider readership.

1.
A vital issue

1.
A vital issue

The local church is the special institution that almighty God has created in this wicked and rebellious world, to glorify our Lord Jesus Christ. The world follows Satan. His wickedness and influence are felt in all human and earthly institutions, but the local church belongs to Christ and its primary task is to stand for him and to exalt his glorious name in an hostile environment of unbelieving sinners. The church is called to show forth the praises of him who has called us out of darkness into his marvellous light. Angels and glorified saints worship God in heaven, the local church worships and adores him on earth. We can only marvel at the tremendous privilege God has extended to his people on earth. In the eternal glory, we shall doubtless praise him for it. While still in this world, however, if churches are truly to show forth his praises they must live in obedience to his word. Plainly, if a church, in its life and practice ignores the requirements of scripture through disobedience or ignorance it cannot fulfil its high calling. It must diligently search the scriptures to know the mind of the Lord.

In addition, we understand that the local church is God's special instrument in the world for the furtherance of his kingdom. All Christian activity should issue from it – missionary works at home or abroad, ministry to believers, works of compassion and Christian charity. Preachers, evangelists, church officers should emerge from the local fellowship of the saints and that same fellowship should be the pure and healthy environment within which Christians live, progress and develop in spiritual things. All this further stresses the vital importance of maintaining the church according to the word of God.

It is not surprising that Satan and his hosts are set upon the destruction of churches. He hates them and is far more concerned to undermine them and destroy their testimony than merely to trouble individual Christian lives. When a believer yields to temptation it brings dishonour to the Lord and sad consequences for the individual and others connected with him. When a church breaks down or departs from the truth it is impossible to judge how far-reaching the effects might be. Many a town and village in Britain seems to have closed to the Gospel for 50 years or more because a once-thriving and influential church in the locality was torn by internal strife or caught up in a public scandal that has become common knowledge. How we must watch and pray over the churches, recognising that we can only really combat the enemy if we understand the scriptures. We have also to confess that in many churches, the work of the gospel is proceeding painfully slowly. We find often that only a minority of the members are truly active, the majority are not really involved and do not understand the responsibilities of church membership. Sometimes the leadership is weak or the leaders may be finding it impossible to exercise their biblical function because the members are refusing them their authority. Some situations lack any attempt at church discipline and others may be grievously weakened and compromised through connections with other churches that have departed from the word of God.

When, however, a church lives and acts according to the scriptures with the power and blessing of the Holy Spirit, it becomes something beautiful. God is honoured by its witness and it is truly invincible in the world. Those who love the Lord rejoice to be part of such a church and gladly commit themselves wholeheartedly in fellowship, prayer, service and material giving. The biblical church will face problems and trials but heaven's blessing will be felt and there will be a fragrance and fruitfulness in all that it undertakes. Let us therefore turn to God's word and learn afresh of his purposes for the church.

2.
The nature
of the local church

2.
The nature of the local church

Before considering how the Lord would have us conduct the life of the church we must discover exactly what the Bible teaches about the church itself. Some confusion has developed during the past 100 years among nonconformists partly because of the appearance of the Christian societies and movements (Missionary Societies, Christian Unions, etc.) which have no doubt been greatly used of God but have not placed great emphasis on New Testament local church teaching. Consequently, some people take the view that the local church is merely a convenient association of like-minded believers who manage their affairs democratically with everyone having an equal right to control the business of the church. Others take an even weaker view than that and decline to be formally associated with any local Church. They are satisfied to attend services wherever it takes their fancy, to move around and never commit themselves to any specific company of the Lord's people. Such have no substantial view of the local church, at all.

Then there is another weak and dangerous attitude that creeps back regularly among evangelicals. It seems to stem from a lack of confidence in the power of the Holy Spirit working in the midst of the local church and says that when churches gather into denominational structures, their combined effectiveness is greater than their total effectiveness if they had remained independent. It is then an easy step to tolerate association and fellowship with 'churches' that are not faithful to Scripture.

When then is the local church in the purpose of almighty God? We understand that Christ has his universal Church and that it consists of all his blood-bought people. It is the Bride of Christ, the New Jerusalem. However, frequently in the New Testament it is quite difficult to discover if a particular passage refers to the local church or the universal Church. The same Greek word is used (e.g. I Timothy 3:15) and the 'Church' is often called the 'Church of God', or the 'Church of the

Living God'. The point is that the universal Church, in this present age, is truly represented by the local church. We may look at a genuine local, gospel church and say, 'Here is Christ's church, the true body of Christ; it is not merely part of it, it is **the Church**'. Thus in Acts 13:1 we have: '**the church** that was at Antioch', and in I Corinthians 1:2 '**the church** of God which is at Corinth'. Any true local church, therefore, is the present-day manifestation of the universal Church. It has Christ as its head and is to be a God-honouring, Christ-glorifying, Spirit-created body of the Lord's people. For Christians to decline to be associated and committed to a local church is for them to deny the purposes of God in redeeming a bride for his Son.

It is upon this basic fact, that the local church is the true and temporary manifestation of the universal Church, that we are able to establish our church life and practice. It is very precious and far-reaching and it greatly elevates the status of the local church in our understanding.

The church at Antioch

Following the death of Stephen, there was great persecution against the 'church which was at Jerusalem' (Acts 8:1) and Christians had to flee to many places. Wherever they went, they preached the gospel but restricted their witness to the Jewish communities. However, there were some believers (Acts 11:20) who testified also to Greeks who believed and were saved. The Greeks were addressed with the gospel without any authority from the apostles but by the guidance and power of the Holy Spirit. This took place at Antioch and immediately the church came into existence there. Obviously it was a time of great blessing (v.21) and news of this work reached the church at Jerusalem.

The church at Jerusalem probably regarded this as an aspect of its missionary work. After all, those who had preached with such effect at Antioch were originally members of the Jerusalem church fleeing from persecution. It was not unreasonable therefore for Barnabas to be sent from Jerusalem to discover the true state of affairs at Antioch and to give the friends there such encouragement and counsel as was appropriate. In fact, it is very revealing that an apostle did not go to Antioch. If one had gone we might have assumed that a question of authority or discipline was being raised and that the believers in Jerusalem were anxious to maintain control at Antioch. We might suspect, however, that in sending Barnabas, the apostles were anxious to avoid giving that impression and were ready to view the situation at Antioch as the emergence of a genuinely independent local church.

Barnabas rejoiced to see the work of God at Antioch and readily committed himself to the church there. Indeed, we could argue that he transferred his membership to Antioch because, firstly he worked alongside Paul for a year in teaching the church then, secondly, he was appointed by the church (with Paul) to convey famine relief funds to the churches in Judea (v.30) and, finally, he and Paul were set apart by the Antioch church for missionary service (Acts 13:2-3). We do not even read that he 'reported back' to the Jerusalem church. He saw his duty in encouraging, teaching and pastoring the Antioch church.

Of course, Acts chapter 11 reveals some of the principles of godly leadership and ministry in the local church and we must come to that later, but the story of Antioch is very important because it gives our first view in the New Testament of a properly constituted local church, separated from the Jerusalem church and going forward with power in the gospel.

Why, however, did Barnabas seek for the help of Saul (or Paul)?

Perhaps Barnabas saw in this beloved brother a more able preacher and teacher than himself. That is not a satisfactory answer as it would place the ministry on a very carnal level indeed, making it dependent upon the ability of man. We must always beware of the danger of saying 'If only our Church had men like that, how different it would be'. We must remember that those were the days before the New Testament was written. Of course, they had the Old Testament scriptures but that was all. The apostles fulfilled a very special function in having received the gospel directly from the Lord with the special power of the Spirit in 'bringing all things to their remembrance' (John 14:26). Until the New Testament was written, therefore, the apostles were entrusted with the gospel and it was their duty to teach the churches. Surely, just as we see the absolute necessity for our church members possessing and reading the Bible, so Barnabas saw the necessity for the Antioch church to come under the teaching of an apostle. By this time Paul had been converted about 12 years. He had met Barnabas during a 15 day stay in Jerusalem with Peter (Acts 9:27, Galatians 1:18) only about 3 years after his conversion. During all those years, Paul had waited upon God and had received direct revelation which qualified him to be an apostle. Plainly, that was why Barnabas needed him at Antioch. How revealing that the apostle to teach the Antioch church was the only one who had not been in membership at Jerusalem. Surely the

Holy Spirit is emphasising the independence of the work at Antioch.

We have therefore seen that the local church stands for the universal Church until the end of the age. Though churches may, in godly fellowship, encourage and support each other they must remain independent of one another. Each has Christ as its head. each is a creation of the Holy Spirit to bear witness before a dark world, of the grace of God in the Lord Jesus Christ. Sadly, it was not long after the end of the first century before councils and other governing structures with bishops and archbishops were established that ruled over the churches. This tradition, which is contrary to scripture, is very appealing to our carnal natures but it has been a major cause of weakness in the churches. Those who, in every generation, have held to the scriptural position have frequently been under pressure and even faced persecution for their stand, but the Lord loves his churches, each one is especially his and he will bless where his word is obeyed.

3.
The glory
of the local church

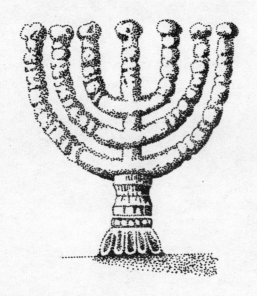

3.
The glory of the local church

The main purpose of this book is to learn from scripture concerning the life and practice of the local church in all aspects of its activity and constitution. We cannot go far, however, unless we bear in mind that the church is a creation of the Holy Spirit and is therefore designed to be a glorious body. Too often, Christians speak disparagingly about local evangelical churches. Attitudes towards the churches are careless. Certainly those institutions which have abandoned the word of God and are therefore opposed to the gospel must be condemned lest they draw the Lord's people into their error. That is a serious business and it is quite different from the idle and damaging conversation that one sometimes hears concerning true churches which are seeking to maintain a biblical position. Similarly, individual members must realise that they are members of Christ's local church because of the grace of God and that theirs is a most privileged position. We need to recover a sense of the glory of the church and, as members of the local body of Christ, we should treat this great work of God with reverence.

In the previous study we learned that any true local church is the present manifestation of the universal Church and that therefore those scriptures which refer to 'the Church' may, in the present age, be safely applied to the local church. In the Old Testament there are many passages which speak of the glory of Israel or Jerusalem and which may be interpreted spiritually. They speak not of the Jewish people but of the Church and, therefore, they speak of the local church. Look, for example, at Psalm 48.

Psalm 48 tells us that the church is to be full of praise to God. It is to reflect **his** holiness. It is to be so full of the pure and delightful word of God that in the sight of the Lord and every believer it is 'beautiful for situation' and 'the joy of the whole earth'. Spiritual men and women should delight in the church and gladly discard the most attractive things of this life in order to be among the people of God.

Similarly, in Psalm 87. The Lord loves his gathered and assembled church more than individual Christian lives (v.2). This is actually very remarkable. We know that God has set his eternal love upon each one of his elect people. Each one is precious to him, each one is purchased through the blood of Christ. Yet, there is a particular and supreme love that God has for Zion. We should therefore accept verse 3 as applying to even our church. Let there indeed be glorious things spoken of it!

There is so much in the Old Testament that we could use. God has declared in an age now long gone that the gospel churches in our age are to be glorious. Prophecies and promises which could never be wholly applied to an earthly nation find their wonderful fulfilment where the church lives by faith under the authority of the scriptures.

The glory of the New Testament churches

During the 50 years or so after the ascension of the Lord Jesus Christ, churches were established right across the Roman world. The gospel spread at an amazing speed with all manner of people being converted. Towards the end of this period and through the apostle John, the last part of divine revelation was given. A series of special and wonderful messages that would sustain the churches until the Saviour returns. God gave, in the book of Revelation, a series of pictures illustrating the outworking of his plan in the gospel, and always Christ and his churches are central. Indeed, after the most exalted declaration of the glory of the Lord Jesus as the redeemer of his people, John is moved to dwell exclusively on the status and state of gospel-age churches in chapters 1 to 3. Although seven particular churches are addressed, it is easy to see that they are representative of all gospel-age churches with their joys and sorrows, victories and sins.

John saw seven golden candlesticks (or, more correctly, lampstands) which he discovered stood for the seven churches. In the Old Testament age, Israel was represented by a seven-branched lampstand, but now the churches are independent. Each is answerable only to Christ who is able to remove individual lampstands (Rev. 2:5) where there is failure and sin.

The churches are surely represented as lampstands because they are called to shine with gospel truth and divine righteousness in a dark world.

It is the word of God, preached by the church that is her great adornment in the world. She is at her best when boldly and fearlessly declaring the truth. A lampstand that is never burning is worthless, and the church is designed to illuminate the hearts and minds of sinners with the Gospel. John perceived that the lampstands were made of gold. This speaks of the great value of the church to the Lord who purchased her with his own blood.

The most glorious aspect of John's vision, however, was the Lord himself. The sight that John had of the Lord Jesus Christ was so wonderful that the apostle wrote 'I fell at His feet as dead'. Although John was so overcome, he retained a clear image in his mind of all that he had seen and we can privately meditate with wonder upon the beautiful picture of the Lord Jesus.

However, we must be careful always to remember that the vision that John saw was of the Lord in the midst of the churches. He was walking among the lampstands. This is therefore Christ as the head of the local church. How this thought should amaze us! The Lord Jesus Christ, who is the head of our church is so glorious in his person and in his power. It is not difficult to understand the meaning of the various aspects of the vision. He appears as king, as the all wise one (this is conveyed by his white hair), as the all-seeing one etc. As we think of the local church, therefore, this

31

thought should be uppermost – it is Christ's church and he is all-glorious. When I speak of the church, I am speaking of Christ's church. When I commit myself to the church I do it in his sight. If, through sin, I bring dishonour or injury to the church I am dishonouring Christ and injuring his cause in the world. As members of his church we share a high privilege and we carry a high responsibility. May we therefore copy the churches of Judea and Galilee and Samaria who walked in the fear of the Lord; and in the comfort of the Holy Ghost and were multiplied. (Acts 9:31).

4.
The membership

4.
The membership

The church consists of its members; it is a living spiritual household of disciples of the Lord Jesus Christ, 'builded together for a habitation of God, through the Spirit'. (Ephesians 2:22) Scripture knows nothing of isolated or roving Christians having no true commitment to any local church. It is the design and purpose of God to unite Christians in a vital bond of Christian love and fellowship, to form local churches. Further, he has ordained that his name should be praised and his work should prosper within local churches, that Christians should develop spiritually and exercise their gifts in serving the Lord and each other within the life of the local church. In Acts 2:41-47

we have a clear picture of the infant church at
Jerusalem. We note the unity of purpose and sense
of commitment that must have existed between
the believers. This is again evident in Acts 4:23-
37, 5:11, 6:1-5.

We must ask ourselves, however, the following
questions:–
1. Who are the true members of the local church?
2. What is the correct procedure of the church to
   follow with regard to membership?
3. How is the life and fellowship of the church to
   be revealed? This last question will be the
   subject of the next study.

The members

Just as the universal Church consists only of those
who are saved and therefore 'in Christ', so the
local church can only consist of those who are
truly converted. Sadly, one method of Satanic
attack upon the local church is to introduce into
the fellowship those who give every impression of
being saved but in fact are not (Jude 4). It is
therefore not only appropriate but absolutely
necessary that the church makes proper and
diligent enquiry of those who would enter the
fellowship concerning their personal salvation.
Those who were members of the church at

Corinth were 'sanctified in Christ Jesus, called to be saints' (I Corinthians 1:2). The church at Ephesus is described as 'the saints which are at Ephesus' and, 'faithful in Christ Jesus'.

The Lord Jesus said (in Matthew 18:17) that if anyone refuses to hear and receive admonition from the church, 'let him be unto thee as an heathen man and a publican'. This is further emphasised in 1 Corinthians 5:4-5. We shall deal with church discipline later but the point to be made at present is that the church must regard the heathen (or unbeliever) as quite outside its life and fellowship. It is obvious, therefore, that we must ensure as far as possible that only truly converted people are accepted as members.

Then from I Corinthians 12:13 we learn that it is the gracious work of the Spirit uniting saved souls with the church. Paul used the expression, 'by one Spirit are we all baptised into one body'. This baptism is the invisible work of the Holy Spirit but it is undoubtedly to be demonstrated in the ordinance of believer's baptism. Acts 2:41 illustrates the correct order. Firstly, receiving the word of the gospel; secondly, being baptised; and thirdly, being added to the church. We declare, therefore, that church members must be believers who have been baptised. It is interesting to note that even those who practice infant baptism would say that a person cannot be a member of the

37

church without baptism.

In I Corinthians Chapter 12, Paul used the idea of a physical body to describe the life of the church. Each member is like a part of the body and cannot be independent of any other part. Every part is necessary and the various parts must function in harmony 'that there should be no schism in the body'. We must see, therefore, that when we join a church we are committing ourselves to living in harmony and love with all the members. There is a great deal about this in the New Testament. We should accept the authority of those whom the Lord has appointed to lead his people, we should be faithfully devoted to the health and prosperity of the fellowship and be those whose lives are honouring to God and consistent with the life and ministry of the church. Those who are not prepared to accept this commitment are not suitable candidates for church membership.

The procedure for membership

There are those who argue that the idea of a formal church membership is wrong. People should just attend the various meetings and share in the life of the church without any special procedure of joining. Obviously this is wrong. We have many scriptures which demonstrate that the church is responsible for its membership. It must be discerning and consider the spiritual standing of people wishing to join. The church is bound to look for a profession of faith and therefore should, at least, have certain members of discernment and grace who can enquire into such matters. Of course, if a person is being baptised and joining the church, there must be a spoken confession of faith in the Lord Jesus, in the presence of 'many witnesses'. One of the real marks of conversion is a readiness to profess Christ (Romans 10:10), and we must expect it to begin among the Lord's people.

Where a person is already in membership in another church, and for legitimate reasons wishes to join the church, it is essential and courteous that there be correspondence between the two fellowships. For instance, it is unthinkable, that someone should be received by a church who is under the censure of his own church. The good standing of the prospective member must be established. In the New Testament, letters of commendation were used (II Corinthians 3:1). This scripture, however, is no licence for the easy transfer system that has been so commonly practiced in many circles. This system has resulted in many unconverted people gaining access to church membership and may well be responsible for much of the decline in the large denominations. Churches are responsible before the Lord for their own members.

Finally, since the local church is to be a body of harmonising members, the entire body should be involved in the decision to receive people into membership just as it must be involved also in the sad issue of withdrawing from sinning and unrepentant members (Matthew 18:17). It is of great benefit to the life and unity of the fellowship if prospective members can testify of the grace of God before the whole church, not only as an additional safeguard against the admission of unbelievers but to establish bonds of love and communion at the outset.

5.
The life and fellowship of the church

5.
The life and fellowship of the church.

So far, we have seen that it is the purpose of God to unite Christians in the bonds of love and fellowship into local churches. We have noted that church membership is for baptised believers and that the local church is to be seen as representing the universal Church until the Lord returns. We must now answer the question, 'How should the life and fellowship of the Church be truly revealed?' In other words, what should the church be doing as a body or company of the Lord's people? For this we can trace out the life of the Jerusalem church in Acts 2:42.

1. *The doctrines taught and experiences shared*
'They continued steadfastly in the apostles'

doctrine and fellowship'. The apostles' doctrine means literally the apostles' teaching, or that which they taught. This plainly means the great and glorious body of gospel truth that the Lord Jesus Christ had deposited with his people. It is therefore interesting and significant that the steadfast continuance in the apostles' teaching was a primary activity of the Church. Some today are arguing that the activity of teaching and discerning the truth is secondary and that Christians should really concentrate upon developing love and affection between the members. The apostles knew otherwise. They saw that the church can only proceed on the basis of God's solid truth. It is not enough for people to cultivate love, warmth or even an atmosphere of 'praise'. God is to be worshipped, his gospel is to be preached, Satan is to be dispossessed and the saints are to be edified on the exclusive basis of God's revealed word.

It is impossible to pray effectively without a developing knowlege of the purposes of God in Christ. Whatever else a church may be doing, however enthusiastic and united the members, if it is a stranger to the apostles' doctrine, it is failing in the most fundamental thing.

Firstly, therefore, it is the plain obligation of the local church to ensure that the ministry and teaching of God's word is properly maintained and that all are exhorted to attend regularly upon the ministry. Sadly, churches in many denominational groupings have missed the point and have sought men for their ministry who have not possessed this vision. Also, the devil is always anxious to remove this element from the life of the church and one result is that many churches have become satisfied with no regular and consistent ministry, having their pulpits only ever occupied by visitors.

However, the doctrine which we teach is dynamic. It changes the lives of the members as the Holy Spirit applies it to their souls. God has made wonderful provision for this process to be encouraged so that Christians might be more able to digest and assimilate the word. It is the fellowship of the church, where members truly encourage, advise or even admonish one another in true love. This is the nature of real fellowship in the body of Christ. (See Romans 14:19; 15:1-2; Ephesians 4:14-16). We continue steadfastly in fellowship when there is mutual edification and support, and there are great blessings in store for the church where this atmosphere exists, where brethren and sisters can truly minister to each other and seek each others' spiritual well-being. Indeed, when anyone becomes a member of the church, the whole church is accepting the responsibility of receiving that person into 'the

45

fellowship'. Thus in Acts chapter 2, the apostles' doctrine and fellowship are so closely related. It should be obvious that where there is disagreement on doctrine, there cannot be true fellowship (Amos 3:3).

2. *The communion ordinance*
'They continued steadfastly in breaking of bread'.

The Lord Jesus Christ has given us two ordinances. The first, baptism, is for the beginning of the Christian life and among other things, signifies our entry into his church. The second, the Lord's table or communion expresses the unity of the church as together the members remember with love and thanksgiving the perfect offering up of the Saviour at Calvary. Both ordinances concern the church but whereas baptism only occurs once for each Christian, all the members should join together regularly to celebrate the 'communion'.

We all are wholly dependent upon the finished work of Jesus at Calvary. He has purchased the church with his own blood and he calls his church to assemble regularly in this precious service of remembrance. This is not the occasion to examine fully the New Testament teaching on this great subject, suffice it to say that the ordinance is only truly celebrated when the entire church is gathered. Too often people have thought of it as a very private and personal matter having no real bearing upon anyone else. Of course we must examine ourselves and turn our minds towards Calvary. Each of us must seek to worship and thank the Lord for all that he has done for us. The real issue, however, is that it is the church performing this act of devotion and thanksgiving and it is only when the church fully enters into it that the greatest blessing is known. See Acts 20:7; I Corinthians 10:16-17. May we exhort one another to show the life and fellowship of the church by gathering together at the Lord's table.

3. The praying church

'They continued steadfastly in . . . prayers.'

It is so important that the church assembles regularly for prayer. There are so many references in scripture which teach that the prayers of the united church are especially pleasing to the Lord. When Peter was in prison and his life was in danger, 'prayer was made without ceasing of the church unto God for him' (Acts 12:5). When the apostles were threatened by the Jewish leaders the church members 'lifted up their voice to God with one accord' (Acts 4:24). We recall the promise of the Lord Jesus in Matthew 18:19-20. When people join the church, they are accepting the commitment of gathering with all the members in prayer.

There are many other aspects of church life, most of which may not involve all the members at the same time. The practices listed in Acts 2:42 are those in which we all are involved and in which we must continue. May the great Head of our church move among us and touch all our lives so that our church will be powerfully and lovingly united over these vital issues.

6.
Fellowship
in material things

6.
Fellowship in material things

It is impossible to read the story of the Jerusalem church in Acts chapters 2 to 6 without realising that besides the great spiritual victories that were being won, the Lord's people were deeply involved in caring for each other's material needs. Read, for example, Acts 2:44 and 45 in which we are told that 'all that believed' (a considerable number of people) shared all that they possessed to meet each other's needs. We cannot ignore such verses, we are bound to ask if there was some practice in the life of the church in those days which today is completely forgotten. Was the New Testament church, for instance, a form of commune? Was it a feature of church membership

51

that everyone put all of their possessions into a common 'pool'?

Let us understand that nowhere in the scriptures is it given that church membership implies a total sharing or pooling of all material possessions. In fact, in the Epistles, there are instructions for those who are wealthy in the churches; those who possessed slaves etc., as compared with those who happened to be slaves. It is never assumed that everyone would enjoy a common standard of living.

To understand Acts 2:44 and 45 we must first remember that it is an essential mark of true, saving grace that a child of God truly loves and cares for his (or her) fellow believers. This is the great issue of Matthew 25:31-46. There is no such thing as a Christian who can ignore the pressing needs of a brother or sister in the Lord. This point is made so frequently in the Bible. If someone claims to be converted and is unmoved by the needs of other Christians, his claim is false.

Obviously then, with so many being truly saved on the day of Pentecost and in the weeks that followed, there was awakened within many hearts something that must have been almost unknown in first century society, a deep compassion for the needy in the fellowship.

Not only was the Holy Spirit creating this as a result of the new birth, but also the apostles would certainly have been teaching the commands of Jesus, that we are to love one another even as he has loved us. It therefore became a vital issue in the life of the church. We can easily see, in addition, that from the day of Pentecost the church was faced with a tremendous welfare problem. Presumably all manner of individuals were being converted – rich and poor, healthy and sick, business men and beggars – a cross-section of the society of the day. How would they cope with needs which had suddenly become (through grace) very important to them?

In those early days the answer was a voluntary and loving sharing of their goods so that, according to Acts 4:34, nobody in that vast fellowship was in need. How impressive it must have been to a cruel world looking in from the outside.

In Acts 4:23-37 we see just how vital this caring ministry was. The apostles had been threatened by the Jewish leaders and were told to preach no more in the name of Jesus. They returned to the church which met for urgent and fervent prayer. The Lord mightily reassured and encouraged them (v.31) so that they would continue boldly to preach the gospel. There then follow six verses in which the success of their gospel preaching is 'interleaved' with powerful references to the ministry of caring within the fellowship. It is quite remarkable, as if we are being taught that these aspects stand closely together in the purposes of God. A church which is active and prosperous in the gospel will also be a church in which the members earnestly care for each other.

Surely verses 34 and 35 reflect the great need that must have confronted the church. Generally, one might question the wisdom of disposing of so many valuable assets as houses and land, especially as the church was not itself involved in great capital projects at that time. Plainly this tremendous giving was a response to the very great need of destitute, homeless and penniless church members. Distribution was made according to need and, wonderfully, all the needs were meet.

In Acts 5:1-11 we have the story of Ananias and Sapphira. This was a very solemn and sad incident in the life of the young church, but Peter's statement in verse 4 shows that there was no demand placed upon people to give all their possessions. Ananias was quite at liberty to keep the land or to keep the proceeds. He was under no compulsion to part with anything, but he sinned in that he lied about it to the church and to the Holy Spirit. Giving had to be honest and sincere. Any attempt at pretence would destroy the whole atmosphere of a loving and caring fellowship and would create an undercurrent of suspicion and mistrust that would be extremely damaging to the whole life of the church.

Acts chapter 6, records another problem that arose from the church's ministry of caring for its members. Obviously the great demands of this aspect of church life were placing heavy demands upon the apostles so that one group of needy widows was being neglected in the daily distribution. It was not proper for the apostles to leave the ministry of God's word to 'serve tables' and so they invited the church to choose seven men to undertake the responsibility. Nobody, however, could regard this as a minor responsiblity. The seven men had to be of 'honest report, full of the Holy Ghost and wisdom'. When they had chosen the seven, they set them before the apostles who prayerfully ordained them for this great work.

Even today, the Lord's people face many needs. Sometimes there are financial needs, sometimes problems of employment, difficulties of housing young people and caring for the elderly. Churches should always be alert to the needs of individual members and accept joyfully the responsibility of sharing, in a genuine attitude of love and fellowship.

'As we have therefore opportunity, let us do good unto all men, especially unto them who are of the household of faith' (Galatians 6:10).

7.
The church
and its government

7.
The church and its government

How should the local church be governed? How should decisions be taken and proper order in the life of the church be maintained? Who is responsible for ensuring a well-balanced and comprehensive ministry throughout the church? The whole question of church government and order must be examined in the light of scripture. It has extremely far-reaching consequences and is certainly not a matter of personal taste or preference. Since Christ is the great Head of the local church it would be extremely surprising if he left nothing in his word showing how the affairs of his body on earth were to be managed. Even so there are those who look at the great differences in this regard, between various denominational practices, and say that it is a matter of indifference to the Lord.

It is worth noting the tremendous differences that exist between denominations with regard to church government (or order). At one extreme is the 'Anglican' (or Episcopal) order whereby the affairs of the churches are controlled by bishops. Within a diocese, the bishop is the head of the church structure and all are answerable to him. Plainly this type of church order has been handed down from the Catholic tradition and it certainly emerged very early in church history. However, we contend that it is not biblical but traditional. At the other extreme is the 'Congregational' order which maintains that all members have equal responsibility in deciding and directing the affairs of the church. Pastors, elders and deacons are, therefore, completely answerable in all that they do, to the church members' meeting. The church operates democratically with, hopefully, the majority view expressed at the church meeting reflecting the will of God. Since most English Congregationalists abandoned their position when they united with the English Presbyterians to form the 'United Reformed Church', the Congregational order is most evident today in General Baptist and Independent Evangelical Churches. It does not, however, precisely fit the scriptural pattern nor does it agree with the historic 1689 Baptist Confession of Faith.

Many Christians believe that as church members, they have an automatic right to bring any issue to the vote at a church meeting. Where this is denied to them they become indignant and suspicious that an authoritarian structure (such as the Episcopal order) is being imposed upon them. They may simply suspect (like Korah in Numbers 16:3) that their leaders are taking too much upon themselves.

What then does the word of God teach? Is it the Congregational order with every member potentially involved in every decision? To look at it another way, does the Lord give gifts of leadership and spiritual oversight that must be exercised at the expense of the authority of the church meeting? If there are those whom the Lord has raised up to lead his people, then the church would be sinning if it failed to follow their leadership. Similarly, if God-ordained leaders failed to exercise their gifts in leading the people of God they also would be guilty of sin.

Elders in the churches

When Paul was on his way back to Jerusalem and facing certain imprisonment, he had one last opportunity of communicating with the beloved Ephesian church. We read (Acts 20:17) that he called for the 'elders' of the church and gave them this instruction:

> 'Take heed therefore unto yourselves, and to all the flock, over the which the Holy Ghost hath made you overseers, to feed the Church of God, which he hath purchased with his own blood' (Acts 20:28).

There are two words mentioned here which require special attention. The word 'elder' in Acts 20:17 is the Greek word *'presbuteros'*. In I Timothy 4:14 the assembly of church elders is translated 'presbytery'. The word 'overseer' is a translation from the Greek word *'episkopos'*. In various other passages *'episkopos'* is rendered as 'bishop'.

Obviously we can immediately dispense with the idea that a 'bishop' or *'episkopos'* in the New Testament had authority over a number of churches. There were an unspecified number in the Ephesian church alone. Also we may safely conclude that 'elders' *(presbuteros)* were, in fact, 'overseers' *(episkopos)* of the local church. Really the first word is a title, the second is what they had to do.

In I Peter 5:1 Peter specifically encourages the elders using the word *'presbuteros'*. He says that he is a 'fellow elder' and he calls upon them to feed the flock of God. The actual words are 'to shepherd' the flock of God. Moreover, they are gladly and sincerely to exercise the oversight, not in a domineering way but as wise examples leading the people of God forward.

There are many other references to elders and overseers and it is very easy to see therfore that God is pleased to establish those within the Churches who must lead and shepherd the people of God. This implies therefore that some must carefully, lovingly and humbly exercise real authority, being responsible primarily not to the church meeting but to the chief shepherd (I Peter 5:4). Similarly, the church must humbly accept this authority (v.5) and follow the leading.

Consider I Timothy 5:17. Elders are required to 'rule well' and in I Timothy 3:5 we infer that they are to 'take care' of the church of God. In Hebrews 13:17 we are told to 'obey them that have the rule over you'. It must be admitted that these requirements are almost wholly neglected in the churches today. One hears of church members criticising their pastor or elders for very small matters–and picking and choosing over what parts of the ministry they are prepared to accept. Similarly, one recognises that many churches seem devoid of real leadership, whether because the 'overseer(s)' have abdicated their responsibility or because the church is so organised that it believes that in all things the will of the church meeting is paramount. Many a pastor or elder would find it a sobering and salutory experience if the churches were to show responsive attitudes to the leadership.

Who are the Elders?

Titus was a worker in the gospel alongside Paul. In Titus 1:5 we read that Paul required Titus to appoint elders throughout all the cities of Crete – men of very good standing whose qualities were widely acknowledged to be God-honouring. They had to hold fast the 'faithful word' so that with sound doctrine they could exhort and convince those who, in the church, were acting or speaking in error. I Timothy 3:1-7 also describes the qualities of an overseer.

In the various references mentioned above, the overseers or elders are required to feed or shepherd the flock of God. Paul especially mentions the elders 'who labour in the word and doctrine' (I Timothy 5:17). The most significant activity of the elders is in the ministry of the word of God, and according to this verse this is such a special work as to make those engaged upon it distinctly set apart (i.e. those known today as

'Pastors'). Some churches have appointed several elders and have declared that the minister of God's word is just one of this group, 'the preaching elder'. This is wrong, we should have such a high esteem for the word of God that we highly honour the office of the pastor and teacher. On the other hand, if the Lord raises up other men who are spiritual, fulfilling the conditions of I Timothy 3:1-7 and are able to lead, exhort and advance the life of the church, to watch over and care for the people of God, then the church must recognise them and gladly submit to their authority.

It is therefore necessary for the church to be aware of spiritual gifts in its membership. If a brother is highly esteemed and effective in handling and applying God's word so as to uphold and lead the people, he should be set apart by the church as an 'elder'. Sometimes great grace is required for members (including deacons) to accept the spiritual authority of elders – to accept that there are those even from among them who are to be seen as leaders. Where everything is done in love and with the blessing of God, the result is much prosperity in the church.

8.
Elders, their appointment and duties

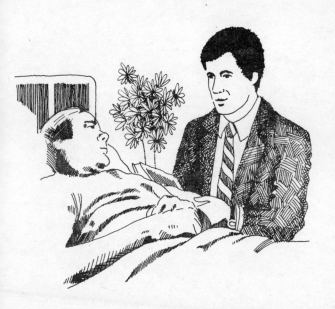

8.
Elders, their appointment and duties

One of the most difficult questions to solve by reference to the New Testament is 'Who actually appoints the elders of the church?'. In Acts 14:23 we find Paul and Barnabas 'ordaining' or 'appointing' elders in every church. Plainly, although the churches in Lystra, Iconium and Antioch were very young and there could hardly have been many mature believers among them, the need for leadership was so pressing that the Holy Spirit soon raised up those who were fitted for this great responsibility. Given, however, the great respect that the apostles had for the independence of the local church, what was the basis of Paul's authority that he should appoint elders in the churches? In the same way, how could Paul instruct Titus to ordain elders in every city of Crete (Titus 1:5)? There seems to be no particular passage of the New Testament specifically detailing the procedure.

We must, of course, recognise that Acts chapter 14 and Titus chapter 1 describe missionary situations in very unusual circumstances. For instance, no New Testament was available for the young churches to draw upon, and so the direct guidance and wisdom of an apostle were necessary. Also, it was miraculous that in so short a time people emerged fitted for the task. Perhaps it required the special ministry of an apostle (or his representative) to discern the mind of the Lord in this matter. Normally, those who had only recently been converted would not be considered for the office (I Timothy 3:6).

In our day the more common situation is that of a church which would already have one or more elders. There would be those therefore already leading the fellowship in spiritual matters. Obviously such men would have to exercise their leadership in proposing the recognition of a certain brother as an elder or even perhaps in explaining, from scripture, why it would be wrong to appoint someone else to the office. That does not mean that elders are appointed by elders, it is just that the God-ordained leaders of the church are bound to exercise leadership in this mater also. Scripture requires that the church members honour and willingly submit to the elders, acknowledging that the Lord has raised up such men. It is obvious, therefore, that there should be a clear recognition throughout the entire church that a particular brother is God's man for this office. Elders, deacons and church members should be of one mind in the matter, everyone should be gladly consenting to the appointment or else they will not be truly ready to accept his authority (Hebrews 13:7,17).

Qualifications of an elder

One would expect that a person would be set apart as an 'elder' or 'overseer' who had already emerged as a leader in the work of Christ's church. People would have been influenced and blessed through his life and service for the Lord Jesus before any decision had been taken concerning the eldership. It should go without saying that nobody is appointed to such an office as a reward for faithful service in some other capacity or simply through having been a church member for a long time. Churches obviously need spiritual men, gifted of God to lead them.

Even when a person has clearly emerged as spiritual and has been an influence for great good

71

in the church, it is necessary to test his life against the requirements of scripture – I Timothy chapter 3 and Titus chapter 1. We remind ourselves that the word 'bishop' is really the word 'overseer' and applies specifically to elders. It is easy to see how most of these qualities apply generally to spiritual men, but it is conceivable, for example, that a man, otherwise so suitable, would be disqualified because he was unable to rule his own household. It may not be altogether his fault, but he may have unbelieving and unruly children or other family problems that would make it quite impossible for him to hold office as an elder.

It may also be that, although he has a good reputation in the church, the world generally has him in low esteem. Of course, spiritual men expect to face persecution and slander from the world but this is not quite the same as being of bad reputation in the world (I Timothy 3:7). Sadly it is also possible for a man to possess certain defects which, in love, the church may be tempted to overlook – for example, in spite of everything he may become angry very easily (Titus 1:7), or display an impatient attitude.

The calling to eldership is very serious indeed. A man may render the most valuable and spiritual service in the church and yet be disqualified from this office.

The appointment of elders

A church should realise that when it appoints an elder, it is setting a man apart for a great work and that he will need the continual prayers of the Lord's people and special and continual anointing of the Holy Spirit. When Paul and Barnabas appointed elders (Acts 14:23) they made it a matter of much prayer accompanied by fasting. The church should gather for a special time of worship, prayer and ministry that the blessing of God might be upon this serious but joyful matter.

The duties of elders

The church is the environment within which the Lord's people grow in grace and from which the gospel is proclaimed. It is as the people pray and the word of God is preached that Christ's kingdom prospers. The elders have to lead the church in this great work.

They are supremely concerned that the word of God is proclaimed to believers and unbelievers. There must be among the elders the 'Pastor' whose main responsibility is to 'labour in the word and doctrine'. This must be a distinct office. God calls the pastor to devote himself to preaching and

73

teaching the scriptures (Ephesians 4:11).

However, the elders generally will be concerned as to how individuals are receiving the word and applying it to their own lives in all the various circumstances that Christians must face. Elders must have a deep love and respect for all the Lord's people and be able graciously to exhort, direct, encourage, teach and sometimes rebuke. They must be able to deal patiently and firmly, with love and wisdom as the situation demands.

They must also be constantly reviewing the gospel witness of the church, looking for fresh opportunities and directing the church forward in its evangelism. They must be men of prayer, vision and faith, ever promoting the cause of Christ.

This is a great work in which there is need for continued dependence upon the blessing of the Holy Spirit. May the Lord give his church worthy elders in these days.

9.
Deacons in the church

9.
Deacons in the church

The Lord has made all necessary provision that his local churches should be well-ordered and properly maintained. We considered in a previous chapter the caring ministry of the church and saw that in New Testament times the church shouldered a great welfare burden. Many of the members were in great need, and so, those people who were able, freely gave of their possessions to meet the situation. The apostles found that the administration of the welfare supplies was time consuming and that they were, as a result, in danger of abandoning their vital ministry in the word of God. They solved the problem by asking the church to choose out seven spiritual and honourable men whom they might appoint over this business. Thus the apostles would be completely relieved of this work and would give themselves continually to prayer, and to the ministry of the word (Acts 6:4). This is almost certainly the origin of the office of 'deacon'. The word 'deacon' is derived from the Greek word for 'service' which is used in Acts 6:1 and translated 'ministration'.

In Philippians 1:1 Paul and Timothy greet all the church members at Philippi, then the 'overseers' and finally the deacons. It would not be unreasonable in this verse to translate the word 'deacons' as 'those who serve'. In I Timothy 3:8 exactly the same word is used for 'deacons', but in both references it is quite clear that Paul has a special office, quite distinct from the elders, in mind. Of course the same Greek word is translated elsewhere in scripture as ministry, but there the context makes it plain that the idea of 'one who serves' is being used to emphasize that the preaching of the gospel is serving the spiritual welfare of men and women.

From I Timothy 3:8-13 we may infer that deacons are to be greatly trusted and respected by the church and that their work is of great value in the kingdom of God.

What then is their responsibility? Deacons are men whom the church trusts to administer its material affairs. Stephen and the other brethren were trusted with the colossal task of administering the welfare and caring ministry of the church. They were placed over the business. The distribution of resources was entirely in their hands and everyone was happy to leave it with them. Because they were spiritual men of good reputation, the church accepted their decisions and administration. They were set apart for the task with prayer and the laying on of the apostles' hands.

In our day, therefore, deacons are to be responsible for administering the finances of the Church and all practical matters that bear upon the smooth running of the work of the fellowship. They will ensure that needs are truly supplied within the fellowship and that the place of worship is properly maintained. It is a source of great joy to the whole fellowship when church affairs are in the hands of men who truly understand the needs of Christ's body and the work of the gospel, and manage those affairs accordingly. Deacons should be ready to respond to fresh needs and support the whole life and progress of the church by maintaining all of the necessary facilities. This will, of course, include provision for the Lord's supper, and it is fitting that they serve when this ordinance is being celebrated.

The appointment of deacons

In Acts chapter 6 the church chose men from among them who were recognised as suitable for the great responsibility. So today, men of honest report, full of the Holy Ghost and wisdom, whose lives are in accord with I Timothy 3:8-12 are to be chosen by the Church, set apart as those who are to be trusted. Please note that the Lord requires that even those who are responsibe for material things should be men who have first been proved and hold the 'mystery of the faith in a pure conscience'. It is nothing short of tragic if a church is burdened with unspiritual men of low vision and faith as deacons. May the Lord grant great grace to our brethren who serve in this capacity and may they prove the reality of I Timothy 3:13.

10.
The place of the church meeting

10.
The place of the church meeting

We have considered leadership within the church and have recognised that the people of God should seek for 'elders' or 'overseers' who are plainly gifted of the Holy Spirit and therefore acceptable to the whole church. We have also seen that the Lord gives deacons to serve the people and needs of the church. Both of these offices call for spiritual and responsible men to whom the authority can be safely entrusted so that church members will willingly accept their leadership.

The word of God teaches, however, that the church is ultimately governed by her glorious Head, the Lord Jesus Christ. No individual can claim to be the special representative of the Lord

Jesus Christ. God, in his perfect wisdom and knowing the sinfulness of our hearts has not invested any man with the power of ultimate authority over his people. Church history has demonstrated the awful corruptions that develop when men have taken that authority to themselves.

The Head of the church is pleased to be especially present and to reveal his mind when the people of God assemble in his name. The local church is, therefore, not a democracy (i.e. government by the majority), but a theocracy (government by the Lord himself) where the Lord discloses his mind to the gathered church. It is absolutely wrong to view the church members meeting as simply an opportunity for opinions to be expressed and every tiny detail of the church affairs to be analysed. It is an occasion when the church is assembled to seek the mind of her Head who is with her through the Holy Spirit.

The biblical basis of the church meeting

The Bible presents us with very clear principles that direct us to the church order described above. They are listed as follows:

1. In Matthew 18:15-20 Jesus gave us instructions that are not restricted to church

discipline. He is especially present with his people who are gathered together in his name and he invests his gathered church with final authority on earth. This passage does not prove that every matter should be taken to the church but that the church meeting is the final place of authority. This is one important distinction that separates the 'extreme congregational pattern' from the biblical position. Similarly I Corinthians 5:4, referring to a serious discipline matter, emphasizes that the Lord is especially present to reveal his mind when the church is assembled.

2. Choice of deacons (Acts 6:3-5) and delegates (or messengers) (Acts 11:22) was made by the church, which also received reports of the work of God through her missionaries (Acts 14:27).

3. Scripture declares that all believers are in communion with the Saviour and are to grow in grace and wisdom. Every member of the church is a priest unto God (I Peter 2:5,9), praying and meditating upon the truths declared in his word. The humblest believer has no less a means of access to heaven's throne than the most powerful preacher or leader in the church. This equality before God leads naturally to the concept of the church members' meeting.

4. The Lord himself (in Revelation chapters 2 & 3) addressed the churches. His word is for every member so that when he praised the churches he praised the whole body, and when he rebuked them he rebuked all as equally responsible.

We, therefore, believe that the local church on earth assembled in the name of the Lord Jesus Christ, has special authority in the kingdom of God and, although the members happily and humbly submit to those whom they recognise as overseers or elders, untimately it is at the church members' meeting that the great issues are settled. We must therefore carefully consider our attitude and practice with regard to the assembly of the saints to transact the Lord's business.

11.
The business and conduct of the church meeting

11.
The business and conduct
of the church meeting

The church members' meeting is of very great
significance in the life of the local church. It is
when the people of God meet in the name of the
Lord Jesus Christ that his will is specially made
known. It is, therefore, very sad that of all
meetings that a church may hold, it is the church
members' meeting that is often the most difficult.
In some churches it is so lacking in harmony and
love that people find it a terrible burden. It should
be obvious that if any feature of church life is
discordant with the general spiritual attitude of
the fellowship something is wrong that should
urgently be put right. In most cases, the problem
stems from a wrong view of the business and
conduct of the church members' meeting.

The church meeting relies upon true unity

There is a beautiful picture of genuine spiriutual unity in the fellowship of the saints given in Psalm 133. The anointing oil that was poured on Aaron's head ran down to cover every part of him including his beard and the extremities of his garments. David tells us that such is the blessing of true unity within the fellowship, it runs down like anointing oil from the head to touch every part. This has great bearing upon the issue before us. It is the purpose of our God that believers should be truly united in love (John 15:12), that they should speak the truth in love and be of one heart and one mind. It is much better for me to suffer some personal loss than for the unity and love of the fellowship to be hazarded. If a high premium were placed on the spiritual unity of the church, many of the difficulties of church meetings would never appear.

The church meeting requires an awareness of the presence of the Lord.

When we gather in this way, we should realize that the Lord is among us as our Head. The assembly of the church is just as serious a matter as when we gather for worship or meet around the Lord's table. Our purpose in gathering is reverently to search out the mind of the Lord on issues that confront us, and this should mean that each person comes with a prepared heart and speaks at the meeting with great restraint and care. If we are gathered in the Lord's name we must desire to speak in his name and not in our own. Church meetings have been wrecked by folk speaking from their personal and cherished positions with no sense of the presence of the Lord. The very fact that the Lord 'is in the midst of them' should bring a most careful attitude to every heart. Surely the Holy Spirit is grieved by lovelessness and carnal debate in the church meeting.

The church meeting should deal only with appropriate matters

Here is another source of misunderstanding and trouble. The use of the church meeting to discuss matters which are really the province of elders or deacons is obviously unbiblical, because it is, in effect, denying their office. It is not a case, for example, of deacons jealously guarding their rights, but of the church meeting gladly realising that these men have been set apart for special service. This, of course, liberates the church meeting to deal with the weighty matters of the kingdom of heaven, to search out the way forward in building the church and bringing the gospel to the unbelievers all around.

In the book of Acts we have the records of four notable church meetings in Jerusalem (chapters 4,6,11 & 15), and in each case matters of tremendous and far-reaching importance were considered. Perhaps in our day, the work of the gospel has suffered great loss because churches have deliberated over trivial matters rather than use their assemblies to wrestle with the true business of making Christ known.

How is the mind of the Lord discovered?

God always reveals his purposes through his word. We do not live in days of fresh revelation, the scriptures were completed in the days of the apostles and, therefore, any claim to an additional disclosure of the purposes and wisdom of God must be rejected. Even in the days of the apostles, when God spoke as he did to Peter (Acts 11:5-9), the church looked for confirmation from the word of God that was already given. In Acts chapter 4 the church heard of the threatenings against the apostles and prayed on the basis of scripture. In chapter 6 they decided to appoint deacons in order that the ministry of the word might not be threatened – a clear case of using biblical principles. In chapter 11 Peter reassured the church by referring to the words of the Lord Jesus (verses 16 and 17). In chapter 15 James brought the whole discussion to a conclusion by quoting from the Old Testament with great effect (verses 15 to 18).

This is absolutely basic. The church must assemble together expecting to be directed by the Spirit to the word of God. For example, one member might suggest a particular enterprise for the furtherance of the gospel. The church should then consider how this relates to the teaching of scripture. Is it consistent with biblical principles? Is it truly Christ exalting? Does it violate any doctrine of the church? These things are to be sought with the Bible open. Of course there will be some brethren (probably pastor and elders) who should be especially able to direct the members to the scriptures but all should expect to discern the will of God from his word. This is not to deny the present, supernatural operation of the Holy Spirit who illuminates the word to our minds, applying it plainly to our present issues and stirring our consciences.

We could consider many examples. A church meeting may come under great conviction concerning the commission of Matthew 19:18-20. The Holy Spirit may be pleased to lay this burden very heavily upon many hearts so that the church is led to send out missionaries for home or foreign service.

The great need is for the Lord to lay his word powerfully upon the hearts of the members and to give them true discernment. Churches must be ready to 'try the spirits' to 'search the scriptures daily', to search after heavenly wisdom.

It is very good and pleasant for brethren to dwell together in unity, to proceed in the 'fear of the Lord and the comfort of the Holy Spirit' and thus to rejoice in spiritual prosperity.

12.
The church in worship

12.
The church in worship

The people of God are called to show forth the praises of him who called them out of darkness into his marvellous light. A primary activity of the local church is to praise and worship God. If this activity is neglected all else that the church seeks to do becomes ineffective (Psalm 48:1). It is a sin for any created being not to worship God, but for the ransomed church of Jesus Christ not to be united in worship is unthinkable. Indeed, when a person is truly saved, there will be a natural desire to worship alongside like-minded people. The church rises to her great heavenly calling when she is truly engaged in worship. We are bound, therefore, to examine our practice in this regard.

Forms of worship

Among the people of God, various patterns of worship have become established. In some churches a rigidly liturgical system exists in which the services follow a preset pattern, usually with prayers, readings and congregational responses already composed within a 'Prayer Book'. At the other extreme there are those who look for no pattern or structure in their worship and introduce items in the 'service' as they feel moved. Some argue that the structure of service that is commonplace in our churches is too rigid and denies freedom of congregational expression while others look for much less opportunity for congregational involvement with the use of choirs etc. To resolve these questions we must remind ourselves of the nature of true worship.

True worship is spiritual and scriptural

Jesus said; 'God is a Spirit and they that worship him must worship him in spirit and in truth'. Whatever we do must be consistent with worship from the heart. Obviously the people of God must gather with prepared and cleansed hearts (Psalm 66:18). If a church gathers for worship with many of the members countenancing sin, the worship of the church will be greatly damaged. It should also be obvious that God is to be worshipped for all that He is and all that He has done and will yet do. Everywhere in scripture we see that worship is intelligent and informed. In the Psalms the ways and wonder of God are expressed, for great themes are taken up and explored in worship. God is to be adored for all that we have in his word.

We, therefore, need an understanding of the great truths of scripture and the ministry of the Holy Spirit within our hearts to cause us to believe and rejoice. The preaching of God's word has an important place in worship, that the infallible scriptures might draw from our hearts wonder, love and praise. It is quite possible for a congregation to be so moved by the Holy Spirit as the word is being preached, that from every heart there rises true worship to God. The same may also happen during the public reading of scripture.

We must also note that hymns and prayers, which are not true to scripture, are an offence to God. They may use language or music that greatly stir our emotions but in no sense can they be true worship. They are, in fact, the offering of 'strange fire' (Leviticus 10:1) to the Lord. We must never underestimate the seriousness of this.

Worship has an emotional content

True worship comes from the heart, but it must
stir the mind and emotions. To sing praises to the
Lord is pleasant (Psalm 147:1), and when the soul
is engaged in true worship there is every reason to
be thrilled. There are two errors which have
troubled the churches and spoiled worship. The
first is emotionalism. This is quite different from
the emotions being stirred by the true worship of
the soul. The use of music and emotional stories
and poetry so as to create feelings is to be
abhorred. It is extremely easy to create an
emotional atmosphere with absolutely no
spiritual activity whatsoever. The service may be
enjoyable, it may even attract a large crowd but
nothing of true value is accomplished.

On the other hand, there are those who seem
determined to counteract any true moving of the
emotions. They seem to create a deliberately dull
and forbidding atmosphere so that if there is any
movement of the soul in true worship, the genuine
rising of God-honouring feeling and warmth is
quite suppressed.

It is a difficult balance to maintain. Services are
to be conducted so that our hearts may truly unite
in praise. We dare not seek to stir the emotions
where there is not first the stirring of the heart. But
neither must we quench the true joy and delight

that should come over a congregation as the Lord makes himself precious to each one.

Worship involves the congregation

One of the most difficult aspects of conducting worship is that of involving the congregation. Formal responses such as are found in the Anglican Prayer Book do not solve the problem. Times of open worship in which anyone can engage in audible prayer or in sharing some truth from scripture are also not truly suitable for a sizeable congregation and are fraught with danger.

On the other hand, items in the service in which the congregation are no more than observers or listeners are to be avoided.

The use of choirs in worship is questionable as singing should be a major opportunity for the whole congregation to share (Ephesians 5:19, Colossians 3:16). Also, the minister should exercise great care in public prayers that powerful and relevant lines of thought are followed, so that it will not be difficult for the congregation to follow and associate with what is being said.

101

Worship and preaching

The preaching of God's word in a service of
worship needs to be understood. There is the error
of regarding the period before the sermon as mere
'preliminaries'. At the other extreme, those who
follow a liturgical service arrangement fall into the
error of regarding the sermon as 'postscript' to the
worship.

The preaching of God's word is a major aspect
of worship. It involves the ministry of the Holy
Spirit guiding and empowering the preacher, and
in creating a true response in the hearts and minds
of the hearers. It is a glorious business, perhaps
the most glorious business on earth to open up the
scripture and to apply it to the lives of all who
hear. God has chosen this method to bring his
gospel to sinners (I Corinthians 1:21) and to build
up believers. The congregation should be as
deeply commited to the sermon as the preacher.
The Lord Jesus said 'Take heed how ye hear'
(Luke 8:18) and a worshipping and spiritual
congregation will listen with eager hearts and
minds, expecting the Lord to confirm the word to
their souls.

13.
Inter-church relationships

13.
Inter-church relationships

So far we have recognised the independence of the local church. We have seen that each local church is a creation of the Holy Spirit and is representative, in this present age, of the universal Church. However, we are bound to acknowledge that other local churches consist of brethren and sisters in Christ, in whom we must take a loving interest. We affirm that no church or group of churches can exercise any authority over the local fellowship but there remain powerful ties between all who truly love the Lord Jesus Christ and his word. It is important that we understand how fellowship between churches should be expressed.

The dangers to be faced

Scripture teaches that local churches must be alert to the devices of Satan. Not only does he seek to bring unbelievers into places of influence within the church (Acts 20:29), but he also uses unholy influences outside (see Ezra 4:1-3) that have a superficial appearance of supporting the work. The local church has no control whatsoever over the state of neighbouring churches, but it is vulnerable to the influences of those who have departed from the truth, and it must, therefore, exercise caution in discerning those who tolerate error. The apostle John, who was preoccupied with the need for love between brethren, was absolutely adamant concerning the Christian's attitude to the apostate (II John 9-11).

One of the great dangers arising from strong denominational ties and commitments is that error can creep into a minority of the churches and then quickly affect the majority. We must always avoid giving any authority to denominational assemblies, associations, church councils etc.

Like-minded churches should support one another

When Paul was writing to the Corinthians,

he sent the greetings of the churches of Asia (I Corinthians 16:19). Similarly in Romans 16:23 and Philippians 4:21-22. Churches are to be genuinely interested in each other's well-being, to pray for each other, to encourage and to show love. It is important for us to know how our brethren are prospering and for us to do all we can to assist them.

The church at Antioch sent financial help to the brethren in Judea (Acts 11:27-30) because the Lord made them aware of the great need that would arise there. Paul referred to similar giving from the churches in II Corinthians chapters 8 & 9.

Like-minded churches share in supporting missionaries

Paul and Barnabas were originally set apart for missionary work by the Antioch church. The Philippian church, however, also recognised its responsibility and shared in supporting the work (Philippians 4:10,15). It is quite proper for churches to pool resources in supporting missionary endeavour at home and overseas.

Churches may consult together over difficult problems

One of the most difficult problems confronting the early churches was whether or not a person should be circumcised in order to become a Christian (Acts 15:1). Certain men from the churches in Judea came to Antioch and disturbed the fellowship with this matter. Paul and Barnabas maintained that it was contrary to the gospel to continue the rite of circumcision, but they journeyed to Jerusalem in order to consult with the church there.

Of course there were apostles at Jerusalem but Paul was an apostle himself. He could, therefore, have claimed authority and could also have insisted upon the independence of the Antioch church. The believers at Antioch chose rather to consult with their brethren at Jerusalem in a spirit of love and fellowship, with very happy results (Acts 15:31).

Where possible, and at no loss to the autonomy of the local church, churches should rejoice to encourage and help each other in the great work of the kingdom of heaven. Where serious differences exist in doctrine and practice, churches will decline to work together, but even then they will conduct themselves with courtesy and grace.

14.
Local church discipline

14.
Local church discipline

When a Christian joins a local church, he is entering into a very special relationship with the other believers in the fellowship. He is committing himself to the church, to support and maintain its testimony, to participate in its worship and to serve the Lord within the framework of the church's activities and life. Church membership is to be taken very seriously, it is one of the most important commitments in life. The church member also accepts that the entire church, acting in accordance with scripture and, therefore, seeking the mind of the Lord, has authority to take certain measures against any within the fellowship who are living contrary to the laws of Christ for his people

This may appear to be a very unattractive subject but it should be our great desire to honour our glorious Head and maintain the integrity of his church. 'His commandments are not grievous' and it is most delightful when the fellowship lives in careful regard to his just requirements. Some would say that we should simply rely upon the Holy Spirit to deal with any who cause offence, but that would be to neglect many New Testament scriptures. Note, for example, the judgment of the Lord against the church at Thyatira which failed to exercise appropriate discipline (Revelation 2:20).

It is obviously important also, that we become well acquainted with the biblical procedure, so that if ever issues do arise (and we shall always pray that they do not), we shall act with wisdom and righteousness. There have been cases where church members have reacted unwisely, not knowing the scriptures, in the face of some issue and it has then become extremely difficult to exercise proper discipline.

Sins which call for church discipline

We all feel our guilt, our great unworthiness to be united with Christ and his people. We know something of our own hearts and that we are all liable to sin. We need the constant mercy and forgiveness of God and we cannot take a superior view as we look at others. We freely confess that our hearts are so often cold towards the Lord and that we are afflicted with pride and carnal thoughts. We must be very careful, therefore, to understand the issues that should be the subject of church discipline and approach them in a humble spirit 'considering thyself lest thou also be tempted' (Galatians 6:1).

1. The sin of schism
The devil is always trying to create lovelessness and division within the church. He is seeking to tear it apart. It is, therefore, very wrong when members are divided against each other. Of course, the Lord Jesus taught (Matthew 5:23-24; 18:15,21-22) that we should seek to be quickly reconciled with any of our brethren and sisters with whom we might be at odds. If, however, a member refuses to be reconciled, it eventually becomes a matter for the church (Matthew 18:17). It is similarly so if someone stirs up discord and strife in the fellowship (Romans 16:17).

2. The sin of heresy
We are all learning the great soul-saving and soul-sanctifying doctrines of the gospel, and those who

are young in the faith are bound to display misunderstanding or ignorance. Within the ministry of the church we are to teach each other and grow in understanding. When a member refuses to learn, and maintains and teaches things that are wrong, that person is an heretic (Titus 3:10), and the church is bound to exercise appropriate discipline against him. If it does not (and many churches have failed in this regard), it is not only exposing itself to great error but it is condoning false teaching.

3. *Immoral conduct*
The Church is bound to take action where a member is engaged in immoral conduct. Such conduct is wholly dishonouring to the Lord, damaging to the church and ruinous to its testimony before an unbelieving world. Those that bear the 'vessels of the Lord' are called to be clean (Isaiah 52:11). I Corinthians 5:11 lists the various sins which would constitute immoral conduct. These include fornication and drunkenness, but it is important to note they also include covetousness!

4. *Disorderly walk*
It is possible for a member to act irresponsibly, to fail to provide for his own family through idleness or generally to behave in an unworthy

fashion. This is described as disorderly walking in II Thessalonians 3:6,11.

Discipline procedure

It must always be remembered that discipline is never 'punishment'! The Catholic 'Church' made the terrible mistake of believing that if it punished offenders it would be to the spiritual benefit of the guilty; thus all manner of terrible practices have been followed over the centuries. The desire of the church is the repentance and restoration of the fallen brother or sister (Galatians 6:1-2, II Corinthians 2:6-8 etc.).

The Lord Jesus taught that things are to be established in the mouths of two or three witnesses. The devil loves to create rumour. Christians are often slandered by unbelievers or even, sadly, by weaker brethren. So everything that is done must be on the basis of clear testimony. There cannot be any procedure without this.

Moreover, where a brother is committing sin, the pastor or elders will already be anxiously seeking for repentance and restoration. Where this is forthcoming the matter is not brought before the church unless the whole issue has become so public that it is thought right to bring firm assurances to the church that there has been true repentance.

If there is no repentance the church must address the problem (Matthew 18:17; I Corinthians 5:4), because the offender is resisting the word of God and dishonouring the Lord and his people. Now, the only step that the church may take is to withdraw fellowship from the person. He is to be treated as an unbeliever (Matthew 18:17; II Thessalonians 3:11,14) and so not a member of the fellowship. He is not, however, to be treated as an enemy but admonished as a brother (II Thessalonians 3:15).

In practice, this means that the guilty person is no longer regarded as a saved person. Church membership is suspended, attendance at the Lord's table is denied, he is removed from Christian service. His links with the church are placed in abeyance, but everyone will be praying and longing for his restoration. This is excommunication.

I Corinthians 5:11 does not give the church the right to break up families (as the Exclusive Brethren claim). We would not choose grossly immoral people with whom to keep company, though we long and pray for their conversion. Similarly we would do our utmost for a sinning brother, praying and persuading, but not treating him as one with whose conduct we are happy and with whom we are prepared to associate. We would probably decline the hospitality of such, yet at all times address them with loving and yearning hearts.

May the Spirit of God keep us from sin and may we be able always to encourage and admonish one another in great love.

Postscript

Postscript.

Do not be discouraged! Churches in the world will never be perfect because they consist of imperfect Christians. We grieve over our personal sin, our tendencies to neglect and disobey scripture, our readiness to forget our high calling and to be careless in prayer. Our churches are certain to be troubled by the same failures. Even so, we must strive with longing hearts for perfect conformity to God's will in our local church life.

Of course the work is hard. Many people who truly love the Lord have never been properly taught biblical churchmanship and they find it extremely difficult to accept that their 'traditional' church life has not been quite right.

They cannot learn everything at once and pastors who enter such situations must realise that a major element of their ministry for some years will be to lead the people gently into a better appreciation of the truth.

Beware also the cynics who have decided that virtually all present day churches are in such a dreadful state, they are past all improvement and that although we are obliged to teach biblical churchmanship, we should not entertain much hope of success. We must answer such an unworthy position by declaring that the Saviour loves his churches, he has purchased them with his own precious blood and he knows their sins better than we do. One day, Christ will return in wonderful glory and the whole Church will be perfect, complete and fit for her heavenly Bridegroom. We are all working for that day and we trust in the power of God's Spirit, as He graciously applies the scriptures to the churches, to carry the work forward. Meanwhile, there are times when we are thrilled to catch brief glimpses of the glory of Christ in the church, where there is a striving to follow the divine pattern and real progress is being made under the divine blessing.

We should remember, however, that throughout the history of the Gospel, Christian people have been faced with agonising choices concerning their churches. Here is a matter we have not considered in the foregoing chapters but it must be given a brief mention. Sometimes churches do fall completely away from the truth. There are many reasons for this, almost all of them commencing with an element of compromise that has been allowed to flourish and expand. Simple observation of our present-day situation leaves us in no doubt that over the past century many churches have moved far from the Bible, perhaps in their preaching and the beliefs of the members or perhaps in their practice – their worship and their work.

It must be realised that although we must all labour among our Bible-believing churches to establish and maintain the divine pattern for church life and practice, where the Bible is being denied and the glorious doctrines of the Gospel have been abandoned, there is no prospect of true church life appearing. This always means great heartache for the handful of believers left in the church but we are obliged to associate only with those who believe and practice the scriptures, in worship and Christian service. We must seek for ourselves and our families churches of like-minded men and women among whom we can be committed to earnest and fruitful labour. Sometimes it is very difficult to decide that the situation has become so bad that it is necessary to seek church connections elsewhere; many have had to pray for the Lord's guidance and over-ruling in this.

Plainly we must never cease watching and praying over our churches. We must support uncompromised pulpit ministries, and be responsive to all that we learn from our great Head. May it be said of the gospel churches of our day, 'They were edified; and walking in the fear of the Lord, and in the comfort of the Holy Ghost, were multiplied' (Acts 9:31).